COMING OUT OF A DARK PLACE

A true life-gripping story about mental endurance through challenging time.

ANGELA MAE MORRISON -AKA DARNELL

IIIIIIIIIIIIIIIIIIIIIIIIIIII
I0150012

Kindle   Direct
            publishing

CONTENTS

BOOK TITLE

ABOUT THE AUTHOR

ACKNOWLEDGEMENT

PREFACE

INTRODUCTION

CHAPTERS

Kindle   direct
                Publishing

First published 2023
Kindle Direct Publishing (UK Office)
44 Ashbourne Drive
Coxhoe
DH6 4S

Edited by C. Leckie (USA)
Cover design by Patrisha Boncales

COMING OUT OF A DARK PLACE

BY ANGELA MAE MORRISON-AKA DARNELL

ABOUT THE AUTHOR

Angela Morrison is a registered nurse by profession. She works part-time, but writing has always been her passion. She published her first book in February 2022, "My weight-loss journey through lockdown 2020". It tells of her challenging weight loss experience during the pandemic. The author lives in the UK/Birmingham with her husband Roy and children.

ACKNOWLEDGEMENTS

I WOULD LIKE TO SAY SPECIAL THANKS TO THE FOLLOWING PEOPLE: -

Dalmar my son for allowing me to write this book **"COMING OUT OF A DARK PLACE."** About his time in this "dark place", sharing his feelings, the good the bad times and the worse times. He is now out of that dark place and sharing his experience with you.

My daughter Jamila and my younger son Ryan who continues to give their love and support to their brother and the rest of the family.

My family in America my mom, my brothers, and sisters, for their continue love and support to me and the kids. Also, a special thanks to my sister Vanetta (DR. V.G. Hyatt) otherwise called Shem and Claudette who were very instrumental in helping to proofread my book.

And finally, to my husband Roy Morrison who is a tower of strength, he is always there to support and encourage me in whatever I do. Being the family chauffeur driving me and the kids wherever we wanted to go.

"COMING OUT OF A DARK PLACE"

BY ANGELA MAE MORRISON- AKA DARNELL.

Coming out of a dark place tells the true story of Dalmar a teenage boy (The author's son) who became practically housebound for over two and a half years, due to a bad attack of eczema. This skin disease severely affected his entire body, causing him deep stress and depression. The physical impact was so extensive that it prevented him from performing his part-time job, and worse, it threatened to destroy his dream of playing football as a career.

The emotional toll on him got more devastating as he moved from doctor to doctor without any improvement from the treatment prescribed. With the eczema worsening, he was forced into seclusion from his friends, families, and socialization in general.

The flare-up was attributed to stress cause by football and whatever else life was throwing at him during that time. The author talks about the tremendous strain that the aliment had on the family as they tried to cope with the tragic situation.

The book delves into Dalmar's own frustration and inner pain, his struggle to cope with his illness and combat this very stressful and depressive situation that led him into this dark place.

It was a place that was emotional as it was literal. His bedroom was shrouded in darkness, but it was also his comfort zone, the only other place was the sitting room. He felt good in that place, he did not have to see anyone or come out of that place to socialise. He stayed in the darkness even as his skin was getting worse by the minute.

The author talks about the difficult times she her husband and her other children had dealing with him and the situation.

She discussed ways she and her husband, with their patience and understanding, helped him gradually get out of that dark place, which was draining him physical, emotionally, mentally, and spiritually. The author realised that she had to get him out of that dark place before he gets to the point of total hopelessness plunging him into deeper darkness.

Coming out of that dark place, took a lot of physical energy, patience, mental endurance, encouragement, and lots of support from his parents and siblings. The author tells how and what she did to get him out of that dark place. Continue to read about this journey and the gripping end to this experience.

PREFACE

For my son Dalmar the year 2017 was the beginning of his career, he had just graduated from college with a BTEC Level 3 extended diploma. Dalmar had planned to go to university to study sports as well as continue with his football as a career.

During that time, he was playing for two teams one being a semi-pro and the other being a Sunday league as a defender. Dalmar is a goal driven kid. His days were mostly focused around, football and health. He was also doing his driving lesson with an instructor and was getting tremendous help and advice from his dad. He was also involved with two other football teams, one being Wood gate Worriers under twenty-one, his position at the time was striker and things were going great for him.

Dalmar had a lot of plans which included continuing his university education, as well as his football career. He was just being an average teenager - going out with his friends, having relaxed time with his family/his siblings etc. He was a very happy kid and things were going great for him. When he turns eighteen Dalmar said, "Mom I don't want to have a party". However, his dad and I decided that we would have a party at home for him and invite a few of his friends and families.

Once the party plan got underway Dalmar was in it 100% (laugh) and since it was summer, we got down with some good Caribbean food -jerk chicken, rice and peas, curry mutton, fried fish, mixed salads plus lots more foods and goodies.

A very good friend of the family offered his help to do the cooking. He does very good jerk chicken, so of course the food was delicious.

The party atmosphere was great, families and friends had a wonderful time, the music was great, and we played the famous dominoes games. Often when you attend a home Caribbean party, there is usually domino games for those who do not want to dance, and these games can go on until the early hours in the morning.

The party was a success; everyone who attended enjoyed themselves and got extra jerk chicken to take home. Dalmar was over the moon, and His Nan on his dad side gave a very warm speech.

My mom and my brothers and sisters live in America, and because the party was a bit impromptu there was not enough time for them to come over and celebrate with him. However, they all sent him gifts and good will, talked to him over the phone and via zoom. My son was having the time of his life, and he was very happy, content and enjoying life.

INTRODUCTION

The experience my son encountered is the premise of this book. The reason I said "A DARK PLACE" is because the situation he was in was very dark. He described this dark place he was in as HELL, because everything he wanted to do as an occupation required him being physical and the eczema was essentially snatching that away from him. His struggle with this condition was devastating and a very bad flare-up in 2017-20 left him practically housebound.

This is about his struggle, the stress, the flare ups and his coping mechanisms. As a mother it was very stressful for me to see my son dealing with this changing skin condition, and equally difficult to see him not going out with his friends. Prior to this, in 2017 he was still playing football, studying (on-line) and doing a part-time job, but his skin was gradually getting worse. He had to eventually quit his job and put his football on hold.

Writing about and sharing his story regarding his struggles, and his coping mechanisms during this time will help people out there, especially young people and teenagers, who are going through life with some sort of illness. This could be chronic, acute or mental issues -stress depression or anxiety, or some sort of life struggle/issues that can affect one in our society today. Whether teenager, young adult, middle aged or older adult, they should know that there is a light at the end of any difficulty. However, to come out of that dark place sometimes one needs HELP!

My son could not do it by himself, and he was really struggling. There were times when he wanted to be left alone. This was when we had to come together as a family (my husband and the kids), dig deep and work together to gradually helped him out of that **"Dark Place".**

My book is focuses on what my son went through for over two and a half years, the impact it had on him as a teenager/young adult, as well as on the family. It was worst for me watching him daily with his skin condition getting worse, and just feeling helpless, as nothing was working for him at the time.

As a nurse I've seen many instances of teenagers, young-adults and adults, present with many mental health issues, with most of them been on some kind of long-term depressive medications due to stress, peer pressure, depression or some other form of mental or life issues. It does not matter if they are working, going to university, college or unemployed, it is what life throws at them.

I did not want my son to be further stressed or get too depressed (because he was already stress/depressed due to the bad flare up of his eczema and not able to go out with his friends) or to be on any form of long-term medication. My husband and I tried to do everything we could to help him, so that he would not get to that place.

For me it was very stressful, going to work at nights, working five or six shifts, having gained excessive weight which was leading to a few health issues of my own. I was having my own little darkness to deal with also and it was not looking great for me. My issues, even though some were affecting my health and if left unchecked could be life threatening, I had to ensure that our issues were addressed concurrently. As a mother, sometimes I had to put my personal problems on hold, and along with my husband focus on helping my son out of that dark situation.

No mother wants to sit and watch their children go through hell. It was very "DARK" for him because Dalmar wasn't going out anymore with his friends, and his skin was getting worse by the minute. He just preferred to stay in bed in his room all day, isolating himself even from his siblings. He would either be on the play station or just lying there.

For me it was not a good situation for him to be in so I checked up on him every day, talk to him, advised him, encouraged him, just letting know that one can never give up hope. We used to have regular family dinner and games night, but he didn't want to participate in our family activities anymore, and at times he got very aggravated and upset. I tried to ignore his little outburst, because I knew it was due to the frustration he was experiencing, and that was his way of coping with the situation.

Although he isolated himself from the family, during this time he would still try to find solutions and hoping that there would be a breakthrough. somewhere. He would research medications - cream or ointment on the internet and get my opinion on them. Sometimes I would say, "no don't buy that one", and we would look at others together. However, it was a constant battle for him and us. There were times when he just did not want to be disturbed, trying to be very conscious and focus on finding a solution for the eczema.

Remember, at the time I was also dealing with my own weight/health issues. In my book I talked about how as a family we navigated the situations to find hope in the end. It was really a very difficult and stressful time for me and the rest of the family.

I tried to keep it together, making sure I had enough money to buy any excess medication, hence I ended up doing five-or six-night shifts per week. Being a Christian really helped me remain sane, focused, and maintained my faith in God that there will be a flash of light somewhere to follow. I just kept the faith that he would be better and back to his old self again. I will now take you on that journey about **"COMING OUT OF THAT DARK PLACE"**. Hope you enjoy it and find inspiration.

CHAPTER ONE

FOOTBALL PRACTICE

My son asked me "Mom, can you take me to football practice?" I said "yes" I gave him a lift to his football practice and had to wait until he finished his practice. I was tired, after finishing my fifth night shift in a row; I didn't get much sleep during the day.

It was Monday evening in January 2017 at about 7pm and I just wanted to go home and sleep. Although tired and cold I had to take him, because his dad was artwork, and he had not yet passed his driving test. He was still taking his driving lessons at the time. I took my son to his football practice and waited in the car for over an hour. To pass the time, I played games on my phone. While there I wanted to use the toilet, so I went home because where they were practicing, I could not see any toilet facilities from where I was in the car. The practice field was about 10 minutes max from home so I decided I could quickly drive there and get back to him quickly enough. While at home I ended up chattering on my phone for a little while and forgot about him until my house phone rang. I answered the phone, it was Dalmar very upset asking "where are you mom?"

He had left his phone in my car during football practice, so he ended up borrowing one of his teammate's phones to call the house phone. I told him how sorry I was, and I had a little laugh although he was certainly not impressed. Apparently, football practice finished soon after I left, and he was waiting for over twenty minutes. I was laughing so hard, but it wasn't funny for him because he was waiting outside in the cold!

There were little moments when we would have a laugh about it. At that time though, he was having problems with his eczema, but he did not say anything to me or his dad (he later told us that his skin was shedding and itching, and it was difficult getting his practice sessions in). He also stated that he thought he could handle it by himself.

I would constantly try to help him out during his football practices, however, when it comes to football match, especially when the team played away from home, his dad would take him or on

rear occasions, he would get a lift with someone from the team.

He would continue going to football practice and matches and doing his online studying at the same time. I must admit, at that time I just couldn't wait for him to pass his driving test and start to drive, because that way I will not have to take him to football practice/matches and that would give him more independence, and free up my time (laugh).

When my son turned 18 in July 2017, I took him to the bank, and the money that I had been saving for him in the Junior ISA Account, went into an independent account for him. The bank Teller remarked, "now that you turn 18 you can manage your own account and not your mother." Sad day for me because I cannot keep a watchful eye on his account. (Laugh) I am very pleased, because I did savings for all my kids, so when they turn 18, they can have some funds to assist them in whatever venture they want to embark on.

Dalmar was due to take his driving test, and he needed some of the money to buy himself a little

car. He passed his driving test the first time; this was **October 2017.** We were very happy for him, and I was glad that I did not have to drive him to football practice again, YEA! I was very happy for him; I could get some more sleep and relax, not thinking I must take him to football practice. He took part of his savings, and we went with him and purchased a **used car**. We helped him sort out the insurance, road tax etc however, he had to have a black box fitted in the car to keep the insurance cost down. This is usually very expensive for young drivers.

Even though he passed first time, he got two minor faults, and he was not happy with it, this just to show how he is as a person, because he sometimes doesn't celebrate small wins as to him it just another step in the right direction, just showing a little of his serious nature, but whoever knows Dalmar is aware that he can be the complete opposite.

He took part of his savings and his dad, and I went with him and purchased a **used car**. We helped him sort out the insurance, road tax etc. However, he had to have a black box fitted in his care, to keep the insurance coast down which is very expensive for young drivers.

The black box monitors their driving, which includes speed, proper turns etc. Although he would now be able to drive himself to football matches and practice, his dad and I really didn't have a problem driving him.

We know that now he would be more independent, which is what he wanted. Also, it would free up my time with him, for me to concentrate on other things.

Having his own car and his own account he was turning into a proper young adult, even though he still depends on Mom and Dad for everything, especially finance, but that's what parents do. In general, he is a very independent child. We all know that kids when they turn eighteen, they think they know more than the parents sometimes.

With technology, I would say yes, but for life experiences I try to make him understand that we have been around a little longer. As parents, his dad and I just like to still protect and shield them from the big outside world, but we know we cannot do that forever, they grow up and they make their own choices. All we can do as parents is to guide them giving them a few inches at a time, letting them try things on their own making their own mistakes, and learning from them.

For Dalmar, he knows that we would always be there for him, and when he made mistakes, which he will and have done, we would be there for him. Not to say **"I told you so"** as the famous saying goes but, to advised and encourage him when situations like that occurs, which is more often, especially with teenagers and young adults. Having his own car was a tremendous help to the family because he helped with his other siblings, sometime taking, and picking them up from school. He was more independent, but he was going through a lot of stress with his football team, which he did not say at the time. Although skin was getting worse, he kept it to himself. He later stated that he did not want to bother us.

At his eighteenth birthday, we had a party at home and invited family and friends because it was summer; we had the party outside on the deck. It was a great party. At first, Dalmar insisted, "Mom and dad, I don't want a party, I'll just go out with my friends". We decided to throw him a party, because that's what parents do when their kids turn eighteen, just to mark the occasion. The party was a great success, and he enjoyed himself. We got our friend to do most of the catering; he is very good at doing jerk chicken etc. We had a great night with families and friends.

His Nan on his dad side gave a very nice speech; He later remarked "Thank you Mom and Dad, for having the party. I really enjoyed it". That is the son who did not want to have a party in the first place. As parents, we sometimes must go the extra mile for our kids. It makes them appreciates the little things in life even more.

CHAPTER TWO

THE EARLY YEARS: PART ONE

I would like to take you on a journey down memory lane of Dalmar's early childhood and his teenage years. As a norm, I usually check on the kids from time to time to find out if they are doing okay, how school is going etc. One day my eldest son Dalmar said to me "Mom it seems I am having a flare up of the eczema, but it's not bad." I said to him, "Let me see your legs?" OH, MY WORD! I was shocked to see that he was shedding a lot, and his skin was stripping off. It was horrible and that is when the **BIG problem** started!

He kept it to himself for months, before telling us projecting the idea that everything was okay. He later stated that he thought he could manage it by himself. He was shedding by the minute, his skin was basically stripping off, there was not much outer layer of skin left to protect him from the elements, especially infection etc. His bedding had to change very often, like twice daily and his room had to be vacuumed very often, sometimes twice daily. I had never seen anything like that before, it was extremely bad, I was in shock and I just did not know what to do, I was just stunned.

I called his dad to his room and showed him the bedding and what was happening to his skin and how we were going to handle the situation.

His dad and I started by taking out the rug in his room, to avoid any excessive dust. Anything that caused lot of dust we took it out. We thoroughly cleaned and dust his room three to four times a week.

I made an appointment with the GP and after the initial diagnosis, he was given some 50/50 cream, a mild steroid cream and emollient wash (he used instead of soap) and cream to moisturise and hydrate the skin. The GP told him to avoid using soap, cream or lotion that is scented or includes perfume, which he was already doing anyway.

He had mild childhood eczema for years but never a flare-up and not like this one. At first, we thought it was something he had eaten, or his
clothing, or the washing powder, or dust etc, but we just could not find the answer.

Although Dalmar had eczema from childhood, I had never seen anything like this; he has never had a flare up. At times I forgot he has mild childhood eczema. It was just at the back of his legs and the front part of his elbow, not noticeable and causing any problem. I will tell you more in details. First Let me take you back on a journey of his earlier years (childhood and teenage years). At birth Dalmar weighed 8lbs and 8ozs with lots of curly black hair and a very crying baby.

When I said crying baby, it is not a statement it is a fact. During my stay on the post-natal ward, which was about two nights (because he was born Saturday afternoon) I spend Saturday and Sunday night then went home the Monday afternoon, very bright and sunny.

During my stay in the hospital in the Post Natal Unit he kept crying and waking up the other babies, which I knew the other moms were not pleased about this crying baby during the night. It was becoming very difficult to get him to sleep, at times I thought he was hungry and was not getting enough milk, and I tried to give him the bottle, but that did not help he just continued crying.

He cried a lot although he was breast fed until he was nine-month-old. Monday morning bright and early, I was very excited to go home with my little bundle of joy, and my husband was 'over the moon', I thought when we got home, he would settle down, but I realised that during the night he would start to cry so I just continued to feed him. I just did not understand why he was crying so much and as a young mother, it was exhausting.

Let me explain something, as a baby he cries and cries and yes, babies do cry, but this baby crying was excessively, and I realised his crying comes with a pattern. As a matter of fact, when I was pregnant, he used to kick a lot during the night, I could see the movement on my tummy when he was kicking a lot which kept me awake, but it was joy to feel and see the movement, and I knew there is a healthy baby inside. One day about 2pm I could not feel any movement, and I just panicked. I phone the midwife and told her that I could not fell any movement for a few hours. She advised me to come to the hospital.

My husband took me to the hospital, and she did the normal observation, using the fetoscope to listen to the baby heart rate. She also places me on the Cardiotocography machine for over an hour which monitors closely the baby heart rate, rhythm etc. After that she reassured me that the baby was okay and nothing to worry about. (As first-time mothers we worry about everything). After birth, to my dismay, I realised that he continued with that pattern, he would sleep during the daytime and wakeup at nights.

His crying at night was non-stop, literally speaking, his dad and I used to take turns to hold him. I would say to his dad "I will stay up with him because you have to go to work." This baby's pattern started at 10pm. During the night he would be wide awake and crying. I just keep feeding him until 6am in the morning he would go back to sleep.

I relayed my concern to the health visitor, and she did not have any concern because he was growing, and he was healthy baby. However, she told me to try and keep him awake during the daytime, so he will be tired during the night. I tried that but it didn't work because whenever, I wake him during the day and feed him he just went back to sleep, until 10pm at night. I was a very tired mother during the daytime, not getting enough sleep and not being able to sleep at nights.

Although, during the daytime I tried to sleep when he is sleeping, it was very difficult. I had to do other housework (not much, because his dad tried to do a lot of the domestic work).

The good thing about his feeding is that he was fully breast fed, and I did not have to make up any bottles or buy any tin feed or powder milk for him.

When Dalmar was three weeks old, his dad said let's go to the hair show in City Centre, get you out of the house with the baby and get some fresh air, it will do you good. He said, "okay great!". There was a concert in City Centre that day and Destiny's Child along with other artists performing.   We had Dalmar in the push chair fast asleep. The music was blasting, and the noise was very loud. It was August 1999 and the sound system they were using in those days was a large sound system with massive speaker about six feet high, so the sound was loud and vibrating.

I remember a lady said to me "is the baby okay with all this noise he should be awake", I said "yes, he always sleeps during the daytime", she looked surprised as though it could not be possible for a hearing baby to be asleep through this noise. Dalmar had his hearing test before I left the maternity ward, and it was perfect. That was just his sleeping patterns. My only concern was the night ahead.

CHAPTER THREE

FAMILY DAY OUT

We enjoyed the family day out. It went well, I was happy he slept for the most part, because his dad and I could enjoy ourselves and got to take in most of the show. He did not wake up for feeding. I tried to wake him, but he just went back to sleep. As an adult today his sleeping pattern is still the same, no change there.

As a baby he used to have some tiny pimples on his face and the GP - General Practitioner said it was just mild eczema, nothing to worry about, and based on that I did not worry about it but his crying continued. One night he started crying and I just kept on feeding him, and I fed him so much (he was only being breast fed) in the morning he was vomiting and bringing up milk, so I quickly took the elevator and took him to the GP downstairs. We were living in a high-rise building 15th floor at the time, and the GP practice was on the ground floor, so it was very convenient for me. The GP said, "it's just colic you fed him too much". I also told him about his sleeping pattern, he assured me it was nothing to worry about he will grow out of it.

The crying pattern continued for months, but he eventually outgrew it. Where his sleeping pattern is concerned however, I would not say he grew out of it, because his pattern has not changed much today, he still spends hours at night on his PlayStation, mobile phone etc. when he finishes his studying. Thankfully, that has not deterred him from doing his schoolwork or help around the home during the daytime.

CHAPTER FOUR

THE EARLY YEARS - PART TWO

Growing up, Dalmar had these tiny pimples on his face and the Doctor said its childhood eczema. Over the years it was just on the back of legs, knees, and the elbow. The Doctor gave him special eczema cream and emollient wash to used, which seem to help as going. through primary and secondary school, he did not encounter any skin problem. I forgot he had mild eczema.

He has been on various camping trips and school trips overseas. He has been in various football teams including, Shanley Vipers, Alex Hawkes, Woodgate Warriors, and various other football teams.

During that time matches played mostly on Sundays, both at home and away matches. The entire family would go to football match.

We would meet up with other families with babies and toddlers and older siblings, it was a very enjoyable time for us. In the winter, some parents brought two or three very large flasks with tea, hot water, and hot chocolate, also includes snacks, which was distributed to the families and a small contribution would be made to that family who brought in the food. Sometimes the team would win, sometimes they lost or draw, but overall, it was a very enjoyable time for everyone. At that time, I was also pursuing my nursing degree at the university. At times I was very tired and exhausted from placement, but I still attended his football matches to support him and his teammates. For me and my family, going away on those trips most Sundays, was a very relaxing time.

Although Dalmar played a lot of football and wanted to play sports as a career choice, he was also involved in various other activities in school and in the community. His younger siblings were also involved.

Dalmar was also a member of Scouts, along with his siblings. Coming from Beavers, Cubs, then and unto Scout. After Scout, he went on to Explorer and then on to join the Army Cadet, where he went camping and completed the Duke of Edinburgh Bronze medal Award. His list of activities also included swimming lessons.

Dalmar has been taking swimming lessons from he was six months old, I used to take him to mother-and-baby swimming lessons. The instructor was very good, and he continued his swimming from there, until he went to primary school. When he started primary school, his swimming was great because both he and his siblings were doing lessons. They continued their swimming up to Junior coaching level three.

Dalmar did his life Savers couching level and got a certificate as a lifeguard. He is a good swimmer and still is. During those years, he did not have a problem with his skin, no one noticed he had eczema. He is a very active, disciplined, well-mannered and respectful kid. His dad and I did not have to worry about him or his other siblings when we were not around.

We are Catholics and Dalmar, and his siblings were altar servers at church and baptised in the catholic faith. As a matter of fact, Dalmar did alter service until the age of 16 years, but his other two siblings continued until COVID-19 struck, and the lockdown started in March 2020 which brought about restrictions including attending church. Although at the time, we did not go to church every Sunday, we still went as often as possible.

Dalmar was on the football and basketball team at Secondary school, he also played football Saturdays and Sundays, in a junior league. His interest was always becoming a professional football player or a fitness.

instructor/trainer, having his own business. I always tell him that his dad and I would support him in whatever career path he chooses but "please remember your first priority is your education." I've always said to him "if it doesn't work out you will have your education to fall back on." Also, if you become a professional footballer, when you finish football, you will need your education to get you through another job." Hence, he decided to do the fitness Instructor and trainer in BETEC Level 3.

That is a short insight of his early years growing up, without the fear of eczema. There are times we both forgot that he has mild eczema, there was hardly any evidence, never had a flare-up, it was hardly noticeable.

CHAPTER FIVE

During those time he did not have a problem with his skin, there has never been any flare up or anything to do with his skin. He is a very healthy and very active young lad, also academically, he done very well, on his GCSE. He mapped out what he wants to do from an early age, he said "he wanted to be a footballer/fitness trainer instructor. and his dad and I are just there to support him. We also remind him to keep up with his studies.

After leaving secondary school, he went to Aston Manor Academy, to continue with football and sport study. Just to let you know that he did not start out at Aston Academy, he went to Bromsgrove, which is more like a community Centre, which I will explain later.

I did not have to worry about him I even forget about his eczema. His eczema was never an issue, because it was just couple patches behind his knees and his arms, which was not noticeable. My son has been on various school trips aboard, at Secondary school and at Aston Academy/sixth form. During secondary school, he was playing football a lot and continued with his Saturday and Sunday team, and overall keeping himself active.

At his school Prom that was a big event for him, and he was a little overweight, like most teenagers tend to buy junk food after school, fish and chips or chicken and chips, lots of fizzy pops, chocolate, and sweets and that goes for my son typical teenagers. But due to his height most people would say that's normal weight for him so therefore it was not prominent due to his height. Trying to get him a suit for his prom was getting difficult, because what I like he did not like. We went to several stores but nothing. In the end I just left him to figure it out.

He went to "Slaters" a well-known men's store in the city to get his suite and his whole attire for the prom. The suit came with a warranty, they told him that if he needed to alter it in any way, just bring it back. Prom went well, and he and his friends got a Limousine they shared the coast, he was very carefree and active at that time, nothing to worry about, no problem. That is the end of Dalmar secondary school. He was a model student, well behaved and as parents we were and still are proud of him and his achievement.

Although he did not go to university, as was planned, he wanted to continue his studies online. As stated, he said "mom, I don't want to borrow any student loan and owe thousands of pounds to pay back, the same course I can do online". That was just as he said it, but with a twist, his dad and I had to pay his tuition fee monthly. Anyway, that was his choice, and all we can do as parents is to support him, encourage him and be there for him.

CHAPTER SIX

COLLEGE/ACADEMY PART ONE

Dalmar finished secondary school and was ready to go on to higher education. As parents, we tried to research different colleges to find the most appropriate for what he wanted to do. He stated that he wanted a college or Academy that would facilitate his dream of continuing football and BTEC Sports.

Finding a college for my son was difficult because he wanted a particular college or Academy, that had football on the curriculum, because football is his passion. He wanted to play more football while pursuing his career in sports and wellness. In the end, he chose one that his friends were attending, and his dad agreed to it. It was in Bromsgrove.

The first time I went there with him to enrol, I did not like it. Looking back, I should have gone with my first instinct that something was not right. It was more like a community centre (Club development) for kids with low grades and older teenagers or young adult who left secondary school with little or no grades. My son's grades in GCSE were very good.

However, because of the football and his friend told him about it he decided to give it a try.   While
filling out the forms I was uncomfortable - this is not for him; something was not right. The forms stated something different. In addition, there was no head teacher, classrooms, children, and a lot more that did not add up. However, because of the football and it stated he would have more football time and more "SCOUTS" would come out and see the kids play. (Scouts are person send out to reconnoitre) and they would look for outstanding players, but it never happened.

Because it was September, and it would be difficult to find a college/Academy at that time, I decided he could stay for three months the max and if there were no changes, in the curriculum I would move him.

After a few weeks Dalmar was getting deflated, I asked him why he said, no "SCOUTTING" mom, no one come to watch us played. He was very disappointed, but he kept doing his lesson and his football. Also, he had to come back to Birmingham to play football, he also played for a Saturday team.

He was deflated and disappointed, but as parents we told him to continue to do what he is doing, and not to let that keep him down. The traveling was getting difficult because sometimes he had to take the train, on a couple occasions he missed the train, or the train delayed. Most of the time his dad had to take him there.

We decided that we would try and find another college/Academy for him and let him finishes the term.

CHAPTER SEVEN

COLLEGE/ACADEMY – PART TWO

Back to the drawing board, we started to look for College again, while monitoring his studies at Bromsgrove. Dalmar was going through his schoolwork like a piece of cake, it was not challenging enough for him. Also, travelling to Bromsgrove was over an hour away, a few times he missed his train, and his dad had to take him. Looking back, it was getting too much for him.

One day he said to me "Mom I found a good Academy in Birmingham, it's a sixth form and Sport Academy school. "It links with the West Bromwich Albion Football Club." I said, "How did you hear about it?" He said, "My friend told him about it." I decided to assist him with the registration, and to speak with the principal, (It was the opening day). I was excited for him because he seemed to like this one.

CHAPTER EIGHT

This was another new beginning for my son, finding this Academy, my husband and I went with him to register/enrol. I was very pleased with the Academy, I was smiling, I was thinking "this is the place for him, it is a proper Academy for his age and grade" (not the community centre). Just to let you know, he spent three months at Bromsgrove for the first school term and started Aston Academy on the second of the school term. We filled out the relevant papers/forms etc and waited for the principal to talk to us.

I can remember vividly what the principal said. He said, "why were you in that lower level, with your grades you should be in a level above", he continued, "you will have to catch up but that will not be a problem for you, because your grades are good. Who recommend you to that place? That's not for you. "He was shocked.

I was very pleased and understood the principal remarks because I know my son could do better.

I was very happy he found this Academy to continue his football and BTEC sport. (BTEC level three extended Diploma). He caught up nicely with the rest of his classmates and was studying BTEC Sport Level 3 - Extended Diploma.

During parent evening, the comments from the teachers were very positive and constructive they were pleased with him and the progress he has made. As parents, his dad and I were overjoyed with his progress. He went to Spain on a school trip and was involved in various other school trips while continuing to play football.

He was on the football team at Aston; it was a very enjoyable time for him there. At parent evenings the comments were all good, he settled in very well with his schoolwork. During those days there was no mention of his eczema flare ups. Looking back, Dalmar was doing great, things were going well for him, no stress, he was just having the time of his life.

CHAPTER NINE

FAMILY VISIT/LONDON

As a family, we would go on various trips to America and Jamaica, and, different parts of the UK. Speaking of the UK Dalmar and his siblings would visit their Grand Aunt and Grand Uncle in London where they would spend at least two weeks during the summer holidays. They would also meet up with other cousins. For me and his dad it was great, not having the kids around for two weeks was a blessing in disguise but for my aunt and uncle it was a pleasure having their grandniece and nephews around.

They took them all over London sightseeing etc, they would write about their experiences, and have lots of fun, they loved it. I always look forward to the summer holidays when they would visit again. The family would visit in between holidays, especially the Christmas season, where all the families meet up and I got to see all my cousins.

We would have a wonderful time chattering and just catching up, enjoying the moment as well as the meal.

My aunt was the one who usually cook the Christmas dinner and my uncle carved the turkey. He would give his famous speech at the end which. was always encouraging. He is very supportive to us and the rest of the family. The rest of the family would all have something to say and enjoyed the moment that is what we called a family Christmas. Although we did not get to visit every Christmas because of my job, and sometimes I had to work on Christmas day, we always catch up at other family functions.

During COVID-19 however, no visiting was allowed therefore no big family gathering. I was very upset about this, but that was the status of the country and the entire world, at the time of the pandemic. The country was on lock-down, no visiting or travelling was allowed. I called my aunt and Uncle very often and the odd occasions there was a zoom meeting especially when my uncle celebrated his birthday. There was a zoom party with most of the family. Those were very precious and treasured moments, which I cherish dearly.

After the ease out of lockdown, the family met up in 2021 and we had a fantastic time. It was great to see my aunt, uncle, and my cousins. We talked about our experiences during the lockdown and remembered friends and relatives who have passed away due to COVID-19 pandemic.

The family gathering went well, although some family members were missing due to work and other commitment. There were plenty of food; my uncle decided that he would continue to make it a yearly family function. Although we are out of lockdown, for some place of work mask is mandatory. This is because COVID-19 is still out there and is still causing death.

Meeting up once or twice a year is a very special occasion for the family, and I treasured it very much. Although we are out of lockdown, and some places are not wearing mask I still restricted and limited my visiting to families and friends. I still try to be safe and practical around people because the virus is still lurking around ready to pounce and attack the vulnerable. The good thing however is, the covid-19 vaccine is available.

CHAPTER TEN

HIGHER EDUCATION

Dalmar, started to look at various universities, going to open days, because that was his plan to continue onto university, after leaving Aston Academy. We accompanied him to a few universities open days. He filled out his applications, and he was accepted for a few universities, however, he turns them down, or more likely puts them on hold. Dalmar stated "I am taking a GAP year first. I want to sort out my football training etc".

His Dad and I allowed him that flexibility. While he was sorting out what to do during the Gap year, he continued his football training. He was playing with different teams on Saturdays and Sundays.

Prior to that, Dalmar also made application for the FFC TRIALS, where he was selected and went to Essex for the weekends for trial and scouting. (During football trial Scouts would turn up to watch the players and selected potential players from the trials to continue their football to a higher level of football or football Academy. His dad drove him there and we booked him into an hotel for him for the weekend. This continues for another two week-ends different times.   At the end of the trials, the managers stated that Dalmar had great potential and he will go far with his football. That was great news for him.

Going to Essex for the football trials was great for him, and he takes on a little more responsibility, because as parents we were not there with him, However, I would call him often just to check on him, although one time, I called and there was no answer, and it was late evening, and he should be at the hotel. I started to panic and called the manager a few times before we get through to him.

I relay my concern to him, and he said, "Dalmar went back to the hotel hours ago, he also stated that he was tired and that he probably was sleeping", and he tries to reassure me that he was okay and not to worry, but it's very difficult not to worry especially as parents, I worried a lot about my children. I spoke to Dalmar later and he said that he was so tired from the event of the day he went straight to bed, that relieve all my stress and worries.

At all the trials, he just waited, but nothing came up, because my son states, there was no Scout present during their trials. Therefore, on one was there to see them played, it was just the organiser there. He was very upset, so was I and his dad, because we paid for the trials. H did not let that set back deter him for one minute; he continues to play for team Highgate FC. Dalmar has just turn eighteen years old, and he was playing for the under twenty-one. He was also doing his driving lesson and preparing for his driving test.

One day Dalmar stated, "Mom I've changed my mind about University", I said "why" he said, "the time and money I am going to pay to go to University, I can study on-line and get the same result for the course I am going to study". He said he is going to study **"Personal Trainer and Fitness Level two and three".**

He also continued saying he would save a lot of money and expense, and that he would not have to pay back any student loan, because we as parents are paying for the course. Dalmar said, "I don't want to owed thousands of pounds at the end of the three-year course", that was his choice, and we supported and respected him for his decision.

He checked out a few training courses on-line a few comes with recommendations, he therefore select the one that was highly recommended, which was "Future

Fit" he made the application and signed up for the course, in 2019, (he is still enrolled), and that was due to the two and a half years set back he had with his eczema flare -up, and the COVID19 Pandemic. Doing on-line studies for Dalmar was great. He had the flexibility, and at the end of his studies he doesn't owe any student loan, because his parents paid it all (very wise of him, but rough on our pockets). As parents we didn't mind paying for his studies, because that is what he wanted, and we are here to support him.

As a mother if I don't support and encourage him, who is going to do it for him? I can give him a level of independence, when he turns eighteen, but he has his own ability and thinking, and sometimes I just had to listen to him. As a parent this was difficult, because that was not what I would have wanted him to study. However, I did not want to make things complicated for him. I wanted him to know that he also had a say in the trajectory of his life. I gave him a strong foundation to start with values, dignity, kindness and respect, and RESPECT covers it all. Because, when a young adult/teenager shows respect to their peers, adults, and their parents, that will take them where they want to go.

Dalmar has all those values instilled in him from childhood as well as his brother and sister. I do not have to worry about him disrespecting his teammates or any adult/family members.

After completing his football trials, Dalmar continued to play football, he also started to look for a part-time job. As parents, we advised him to also try the leisure Centre as LIFE SAVERS (since he did the course and had a certificate).   Unfortunately, he did not listen to his dad or me in this instant like most teenagers do, so he got a part-time job at a store/warehouse. He ended up leaving due to the environment because his skin was getting worse.

Not everything in life went according to plan, however, because it was part-time and he was still doing his on-line studying, I just let it slide. However, it did not work out for him and that went horribly wrong.

The reason I said horribly wrong, there was dust involved and his skin was getting worse, so he stated, "Mom I had to take a break often like every 20 minutes to cream my skin because it becomes dry and very itchy".

He also said the supervisor did not like him taking so many breaks, which was quite often. He was going through a lot at that time, but he did not say much. Writing about it now, I cannot imagine what he was going through at the time (it must have been hell for him) but he tried to keep it together, so I did not have to worry too much.

CHAPTER ELEVEN

Despite going to the General Practitioner several times (GP) for treatment his skin was getting worse, and he started to become withdrawn. His skin began oozing and was getting infected (it also carried an odour). His bed linen had to changed two to three times daily. If he wanted to go into the front room to relax, I would have to cover the settee, with extra covering for protection and then vacuum all over again, due to excessive shedding of his skin and the wetness from the oozing.

His dad and I took him to the GP again and this time we asked for him to refer him to the Dermatologist. This he did but we had a six- month wait time. He kept having bad flare-ups, so I decided to seek a private dermatologist, because his skin was getting worse. Dalmar was getting more stressed, deflated, and upset. The whole family was also getting frustrated.

There were times I felt so sorry for him wondering if this would end. I questioned what had caused this vicious attack on his body and getting worse every day, seemingly with no end.

One night on my way to work I stopped and had a little cry and I prayed that God would help in finding some cream, ointment, or lotion to help him. I sat in my car for a little while wondering what to do and how I was going to get through the night's shift. At that time, I felt like turning the car around and going back home just thinking I might find a solution by roaming around the internet for some new and natural products. However, I just shrugged it off and continued to work.

Looking at the situation from a mother's point of view at that time and place, I was so concern about my son. I consoled myself with the thought that he was trying to cope and had family around him. I love my family but at that moment I knew I was also committed to work, and I had an obligation to my colleagues and patients, so I continued to work. At work, I am dedicated to my patients and the staff, and being a professional, I put in my 100% at work.

The appointment for Dalmar at the private clinic was quick, just a week, and even thought it was costly it was worth it at the time. The fee was £250.00 for 30 minutes consultation, and the medication was £89.00.

He was given a very strong steroid, for him to use twice daily for two weeks, an antibiotic cream and additional tablets.

The medication was used only for a short time because what the steroids does is, it started to thin out his skin, and remove the protective skin barrier which caused more oozing leading to more infections. This increased his stress level to high, which was not good for him. He had to stop using the steroids, and the antibiotic was causing him to break out in more rashes, so nothing was working. How frustrating was that? And that was just me venting my anger, what about him, how was he feeling at that time? It was very difficult to imagine, if you are not in that situation one can only offer comfort and encouragement, hoping the situation would get better.

I had to go back to the drawing board and started all over again. (Just to say every time, he tries a new medication; his skin seems to get worse.) Dalmar and I started to look online (Amazon) and other outlets, for new product mostly natural products. We brought a few and some worked for a few days, and then stopped working. Sometimes the new products made his skin worse. It was getting very frustrating for him and so he had to return to the steroids and 50/50 emollient cream. I told him just use them for a short period of time, because it was just damaging his skin.

I remember a time I was assisting him by applying some ointment on his back, and he asked, "How is my back mom?" I replied, "Not too good and not too bad." I could not tell him the truth at the time; his back was like cardboard, very rough, very dry and discoloured (a greenish colour with spots). I told him later it was like "the hulk". We had a good laugh. The ointment was not absorbing enough into the skin, there was not much protective barrier of the skin, due to the shedding and the constant use of the steroids cream.

Dalmar continued to research natural remedies online. He would show me a few and I would advise him on the ones I thought he should try. They kept doing the same. I have been through a few pharmacy/chemists, especially Booth's chemist, that is where I spend most of my time looking and seeking advised on what type of cream to use.

His dad and I stripped his room, declutter, put in air infuser etc. He also had to change his clothing and bedding to 100% pure cotton, all his other clothing were given to his brother or his dad and charity. He kept a few clothing like his jeans etc. With all of this, still nothing was working. I kept talking to Dalmar, encourage him, I told him there is some cream or ointment out there that will help, I just had to keep looking.

He decided to change his diet, because we were wondering if he was allergic to some food, or his clothing or the washing powder, anything. He said, "Mom I am going to cut out meat and nuts for a while and see if that will help." He did that but there were no changes to his skin problems. He continued for a few more weeks, but no change occurred, his skin just kept getting worse. Looking back, he has been having nuts for ages, and had never shown any allergic reaction to nuts, meat, or any other food, he was just trying to change his diet to see if it would help.

CHAPTER TWELVE

At work I would talk to a colleague, who stated that they know of someone who has had eczema as a child and the cream they used to control it, but for Dalmar, it was not the same. His skin was getting worse, despite trying almost every eczema cream I could think of nothing was working.

However, after talking to another colleague at work, they told me about a type of washing powder/detergent and softener (Sure Care Sensitive) which is free of Enzymes, free of Acids free of Fragrance and free of Dyes.

I went and research it and brought it. (He still uses the washing powder/softener to this day). I also decided to wash his clothing separately from the rest of the family. I was just trying to do anything that was possible to help my son. Also, to take his mind off the problem, I tried to get him involved in family activities, but he was not interested, he just kept to himself.

There were times when we would purchase a cream and it showed signs of working and then after a day or two, it started all over again. That was very frustrating. I remember one time I brought a small jar of eczema cream for £18.00 and was thinking, "for sure this one will work" but NO!! it didn't. It continued like that for months, where I would buy cream, lotion etc, and it just didn't work. It was a cruel situation he was in and as stated earlier it was HELL for him.

Despite all this however, Dalmar's mental status was good although not great, because he was stress/depressed because of what going on with his skin. I tried to be there for him at every turn, because I did not want him to go on any medication for depression, due to the situation he was in.

Finally, the appointment came through from the Dermatologist that was referring by his GP. His dad and I went with him on the first consultation. The consultant was shocked at his skin, it was bad, his chest and back, legs feet and neck. Dalmar said that his neck was very painful, and he found it difficult to turn his neck.

The consultant designed a plan with him to provide phototherapy (this uses controlled artificial ultraviolet UV light to help reduce the symptoms of some types of skin conditions like eczema), along with the steroids, cream, lotion etc. Even though they changed the cream, it was just the same result - nothing was working for him. He eventually decided to only use the phototherapy to see if that would work.

The first session was scheduled for a couple of months from the visit. He said that it lasted for twelve seconds. After the session, he was walking like a zombie, he was very stiff. He said, "Mom, my whole body feels like I cannot move." He also had difficulty turning his neck. I remember I saw him trying to get out of the car and walking as if he was practicing for a Halloween movie involving Zombies!

There was no great improvement, in fact as with the other remedies, it seemed to have made the condition worst. All this happened during the period when he was working part-time, therefore he was finding it very difficult to work, play football or socialise with his friends and family.

Dalmar kept having flare-ups despite seeing a dermatologist. He had to be taken back to the General Practitioner and was given the same medication as mentioned earlier. He was advised not to go out into the sun or sweat too much, which he couldn't do anyway, because once he started to walk, he started to itch and if he sweated his skin would itch a lot. Most of his clothing was spandex material due to his sports; however, he could not wear any clothing with spandex material, so he had to change to cotton materials or clothing. During this time, we went to London for our cousin's 21st birthday party, but Dalmar did not attend, as he did not want to socialise.

As mentioned earlier, his skin dried out quickly and he had to be constantly applying cream to keep it moist. If he had to go out with the family it had to be just an hour or less and during that time, he probably creams his skin three to four times within the hour. He was getting very frustrated and upset, because he could not enjoy himself at any function without constantly going to the bathroom to moisturise his skin. As soon as he moisturised it, his skin would get dry and itchy again. That added to his frustration as the whole situation was becoming a cyclical process.

CHAPTER THIRTEEN/PART ONE

Dalmar's eczema and the flare ups began in stages. First it was his legs, then his feet, chest and back and then his fingers and toes, and that is when it also started to get worse. He used to wear socks to cover his lower feet as it was very bad, and the Doctor gave us a lotion to sock his feet into it and then cream it. We did that a few times over several weeks but no result, nothing was working for him.

He practically stopped going to the gym, he placed his football on hold, and he could not go to work, so what was there? It was a rough time for him, his dad, and me but we tried to be strong for him. I did not allow Dalmar to see me having a negative attitude or being defeated, I always said to him, I will find a cream; there is something out there we just have not found it yet.

At times by myself, I felt bad that I was not able to help him and felt like giving up, but I just could not. If I gave up, who was going to help him? If he saw me having a negative attitude, how would it have helped him? And what would it do to him, mentally if he thought his mother was giving up on him? The medications from the Doctors were not working, in fact they made they sometimes worsen the situation. I just had to put on my positive smiling face and continue to soldier on for him every day like normal. Along with his dad, we had to keep it together for him and the family.

I kept praying that God would help me find the right cream/lotion for him. I had faith that God would come through somehow, I never give up hope! There were times I felt low and deflated, because as humans our souls break however, I did not allow myself to stay down as I knew that somewhere, somehow, there would be a solution. I again started looking for other private Dermatologist in different parts of the country, but after a while I decided to try other possibilities as the outcome was proving to be the same.

In early 2019 his hands were getting worse. As stated earlier, it started affecting different part of his body in stages. We just could not find any cream to controlled it. There were blisters on his hands some were on his feet (but not as bad), but because he had to use his hands a lot, the blisters now became an open ulcer.

This time his dad and I took him to the walk-in centre. Although, the waiting was long (about two hours) I didn't mind because it was getting seriously.

scary. Dalmar would wait in the car, because he did not want to be in the waiting area where people would be looking at him. He was very conscious of his skin problems.

His dad and I would sit in the waiting area until his name was called. When his name was called, I went and got him from the car his dad and I went with him to the Doctor, we just sat and listen and added anything that he missed out during the consultation. Although, he was now an adult, he wanted us to be there to support him. He was also more comfortable having me there in my capacity as a nurse.

The doctor was taken aback with the condition of his skin as well as the ulcer on the side of his hands. He also involved the practice nurse showing her Dalmar's hands and asking her opinion on how to treat it. She was the expert in that field of nursing. In the end, the doctor prescribed antibiotic and other medications for him.

I told the doctor that he was given that antibiotic before and after three days his skin would start to break out in rashes, and he was forced to stop taking the medicine. He said he would prescribe a different type of antibiotic and advised Dalmar not to take the one that cause him to break out in rash as he might be allergic to some of the ingredients.

The Practice nurse was great, she did a thorough observation on him. She washed and cleaned the ulcer on the side of his hand and applied a cream that contained small amount antibiotics and steroids. She applied a dressing on top and then she bandaged the hand and told him to come back in two days. He went back another two times and each time there was an improvement. The nurse was very happy with the outcome, and Dalmar was feeling much better with it also. She gave him extra dressing and cream, to change if it got soaked or wet, but told him try to avoid it getting wet. If it started to ooze, he was to change the dressing, which I did for him.

On the third visit she told him he can go back to see the nurse at his GP practice to get his hands dressed and changed the dressings. He went to the practice nurse a couple times, and then I continued to clean and dressed it for him until it healed. His left hand was the worse and he really had a hard time interacting especially having to
use his hand where people had to see it. Even after it started getting better, there were still lots of small pimples on both hands causing them to look wrinkly and dry.

He started to bandage his hands to hide it. Even in and around the house, he would bandage his hands and if he had to go out (which he was forced to do occasionally, especially during the

early stages of his eczema, going to the GP, for appointment etc.) he would ensure that his hands were bandaged.

CHAPTER FOURTEEN

In July 2019 I decided to visit Jamaica along with my family who were also visiting from New York. I decided to give the family a surprise. They did not know I was planning the trip to coincide with theirs. I also asked Dalmar if he would like to visit, which he replied, "yes mom that would be great!" I booked the plane tickets and we stayed at a resort in Montego Bay Jamaica, for a few nights.

There are two reasons I asked Dalmar to come on this trip. One, I am not good at flying (terribly claustrophobic) and needed the company and the second is to give him a break from all that he was going through. I though going to sunny Jamaica might help him with his eczema, as well as help his mental status. Seeing his grandmother, and his uncle, aunties and his cousins, and the rest of the family together I hoped would really give him a boost!

Dalmar had not been to Jamaica since he was a young child, and it would be a chance for him to get to appreciate its beauty and culture. This visit I hoped would help to take his mind off his skin problem and have some form of normalcy. The different environment would be good for his well-being, creating a positive vibe for him, as well as for myself.

Travelling for him was a challenge because he had to take his cream, ointments, and lotions in his checked luggage due to travel restrictions. He could only take 50mls which is a small amount for him, as he usually had to cream his skin very often to avoid it from getting dried. Dry skin causes a lot of skin irritation due to the constant itching.

The flight was a midday one and because Dalmar sleeps mostly during the daytime, (that is a trait from birth) he slept for most of the flight. I would wake him for his meal, and he falls right back asleep. For me that was comforting because he would be stressing me out about his cream, and he would be itching which is not good for him travelling for nine hours on a plane. He did try at some point to cream his skin when he went to the toilet, but as he later stated, "I found it very difficult, and I did not have enough cream." He was only allowed a 50ml cream in his hand luggage, which was not enough for his current situation.

We arrived in Montego Bay, Jamaica in the evening, and it was lovely to be in Jamaica again. I arranged with my friend and her husband to pick us up from the airport. They had to travel a long way to pick us up. They stayed the night with us, and I just paid the difference. It was lovely to see my friend and her husband; we go back years and years.

We stayed at the holiday Inn Resort, it was beautiful, the accommodation was fantastic, not to mention the food, and the staff. The beach and the swimming pool were like living in paradise. For a while Dalmar was very happy and you could see the smile on his face. He said, "This is great mom! I love it thanks for taking me to come." It made me very happy to see him happy, although I was still concern about his skin. I was also concerned that he did not pack enough cream and he might run out quickly, and the worries would start again. For the moment though, I was just taking it in.

CHAPTER FIFTEEN

Being in sunny beautiful Jamaica and the resort was paradise for him. While in Montego Bay, he was playing football with the locals and getting some of the beautiful sunshine which was good for him because a few months before, he could not go into the sun or sweat too much. He still had to cover his hands/wrist with bandage to hide the pimples and blisters, which sometimes would burst and makes it difficult for him.

After various search with my friends, I found a cream which was compatible for him to use. I was very happy I found the cream, as his skin is still fragile and any cream or lotion that was not compatible could just make it worse and that would be a disaster. The cream however, only worked for a short period of time for him to help calm the itching.

We left Montego Bay and went to St. Catherine in a small district called Troja, where we were from and met up with the rest of the families from New York. My sister planned a celebration for her two kids (my niece and nephew) for their graduation from college. Dalmar's birthday was in July and so we integrated both celebrations. The atmosphere was electrifying and the whole celebration was great because the birthday party was a surprise for Dalmar. For the moment it felt like everything was back to some form of normalcy.

One morning while in Troja, I got up very early, the sun was up, the air was clean and fresh, smelling like the country when I was growing up. I took Dalmar and my nephew on an early morning tour/walk in the district/community showing them the different areas I used to play, go to the store etc.

There were lot of changes with the houses and the landscape, but the memories brought back smile to my face. We walked for a few miles and then return home to have some delicious country breakfast.

My brother hired a minivan for the family for us to travel around Jamaica visiting families and friends and sightseeing. Talking about family, we visited our cousins in Old Harbour, ST Catherine.
(Whenever a family member visits Jamaica, we always try to visit the family there). On that occasion however it was sad because one of my cousins had passed away. He was young probably in his late thirties. his mother my cousin was in moaning, but she still accommodated us.

Even at this present time writing this book and mentioning his death makes me very sad. He was always laughing and never had a bad word to say about anyone, always willing to help. I never really moaned his death; I just want to remember him as the jovial laughing cousin I knew and partially grew up with.

I spend a few years living with my cousins in Old Harbour, and that is where I was baptised and becomes a Christian. Over the years, our families kept in contact, by phoning or writing letters I always tried to visit my cousins in Old Harbour, whenever I visit Jamaica. To date I keep in contact with them.

CHAPTER SIXTEEN

Talking about Old Harbour that was my second home when I was living in Jamaica. It brought back smiles to my face, laughter, and sweet memories, especially going to church as youngster with my cousins and friends. We used to go to young people and missionary service; we would walk over a mile to and from church singing while we walked home.

The pastor of the church at the time was and is still a "man of God". He along with the members of the church, his wife and young family build the church up from nothing to the great congregation it is today.

I have not been back to the church for years, however, over the years, members have passed away, some migrate to different countries and others moved out of the community. For the pastor, who is now a bishop he stayed and build up the church and the community to the excellent community church it is today. I hope next time I visit Jamaica I will be able to visit the church and the community.

For me as a Christian wherever I go Christ is always there, so I don't have anything to worry about. That visit to Old Harbour, one of my childhood communities, is memories which I cherish very dearly.

We continued with our tour going to Devon House in Kingston, Jamaica to get ice cream. Devon House is a famous tourist attraction famous for its ice-cream and other food and delicacies. It is also photographic place for wedding, parties, and other attractions. People travel from all over the world to visit "Devon House". It is also a famous landmark in Jamaica. Dalmar and his cousins enjoy the visit and the ice cream and the tour. For a while I forgot about his problems, even Dalmar tried de-stress, relax, and enjoy himself with his cousins.

I tried not to focus on his skin and the problem he is having. I was still concerned about how I was going to get a cream/lotion for his skin but just tried to put things into perspective. The eczema cream we found while in Jamaica was helping so we decided to get some more. Unfortunately, when we went back to the chemist to get the cream it was sold out.

We went to several chemists/pharmacies in Jamaica trying to find that cream but no luck. Fortunately, we were travelling back the next day to the UK. I told his dad to bring us some cream when he comes to meet us at the airport, which he did.

Travelling back home to the UK was very tiring. Dalmar found it extremely difficult to cream his body on the plane, because he had to get up very often to use the toilet. This was not convenient and in addition he did not have the correct cream. He could only use the small amount of 50/50 cream he was allowed to carry with him on the aircraft. As mentioned, the 50/50cream was not helping much, but it was just what he had, until we landed in the UK. Using the toilet on the plane was very frustrating and he found the journey back very difficult. His skin was itchy and dry and started to flake/shed again. Being back to the UK, we were back to square one again.

CHAPTER SEVENTEEN

There are times I really felt sorry for him, but I do not allow him to see it. I just prayed about it and shared my concerns with his dad. Practically every day, I would check up on him to make sure he was ok. I would talk to him and reassure him that we would continue to research possible solutions on the internet including natural cream or anything that could help.

After returning to the UK, Dalmar had another appointment with the Dermatologist, and more recommendations and more steroids cream medications, etc. It just kept going around in circle again and again. I talk to my sister in America to see if she could find that cream, we went on Amazon but no luck.

The situation caused Dalmar to become more depressed again, he missed his cousin's birthday party in London, and it was just becoming a downward slide. I also started to become stressed, but I just kept on going and tried to reassure him that there had to be some cream out there, it's just that we had not found it yet.

The process started all over again. I have visited the Booths chemist/pharmacy a few times weekly just looking for a new cream. I also visited other chemists to see if there was anything different. There were times I brought a few creams for him to try, but no success.

CHAPTER EIGHTEEN

After spending months, weeks, at various chemists/pharmacies for hours with no result, I went to a particular Booths store, in long bridge, that I visited at least twice weekly, and while looking at the section for eczema, I realised there was a new cream I had not seen before. I looked at it and was reading the ingredients and directions for how to use it. I realised it did not contain any paraffin or steroids; it also contains shear butter and other natural ingredients.

I became very interested I the product and rang Dalmar to share the information with him. We decided to purchase it as a trial. The name of the cream is Diprobase daily moisturising cream. He started to use the cream. With Dalmar's skin being very sensitive to almost any cream/ointments and since there was hardly any skin protection; any cream/lotion or oil he used after a few minutes, could start an itch and his skin would be breaking down. I was concerned that infection would set in again, because there is hardly any skin barrier, to offer him any protection. Because of that he was always cold and shivering.

A few hours after using the cream, he said nothing happening, after one day, he said no itching, after two days he said, "Mom, I think it is going to work!" The cream comes in a medium tube, and he used it several times a day. I had to keep buying more and more (it is £11.99 per tube) and with the damage to his skin, he could use up to two tubes of cream per day.

I kept going back to Booths to purchase more cream, I was happy that I have found a cream at last to help him. We could see the improvement; yes, at last finally his skin was inching towards healing! After a few days we could see the difference, however, I kept going back to get more cream until he found out it was sold on Amazon at a more reduce cost. I told him to buy a case which holds about 20-30 cream just to be on the safe side.

It was usually out of stock at the chemist and was difficult to find it elsewhere. Therefore, having too much was a good thing.

CHAPTER NINETEEN

One evening it was around 5:45pm, I was getting ready for work (I started working at 7pm). While sitting on the bed getting ready, I realised that my trouser waist was tight, I was a little concern. The waist was size 22 how could that be tight? I thought. Probably it was because I just return from my wonderful holiday in Jamaica, and after eating all those nice exotic foods (not to mentioned tasty patties) I thought I gained some weight. However, not to worry, I have a size 24 which I was going to take to the tailor to reduce, to size 22 so I just put on the size waist 24 and it fit comfortably. I was not happy, but what could I do, I had to go to work.

I sat on the bed staring in the mirror, looking at my size and hated the image that was looking back at me. I was so sad and upset with my size. I was getting bigger and rounder and started buying bigger sizes and eating the wrong food. My HbA1c
which is associated with Diabetes, was going up and my cholesterol was increasing. Both my knees were

very painful and stiff, for which I was getting steroids injection every six months.

Although I was a gym member, it was very difficult to get to the gym after working five and sometimes six nights weekly. When I finished work in the mornings, I was very tired especially after the fifth night, so going to the gym I do not have any energy left. I tried to visit the gym often as I could, sometimes once weekly or every two weeks, which was not good enough. I tried to walk, but I did not have the time. At that time, I felt very deflated and defeated with my weight.

Over the years I have tried several weight-loss programmes, different diets and sought professional help from my GP but nothing was working. With all those thoughts going through my head, feeling sorry for myself, and thinking, what was I going to do? When I heard a voice shouted said "Mom! Mom! Come here please".

Well, that got me back to reality, it was my son, I went into his room and asked, "what is it son?" he said, "Look at my face and my head?" What I see was not scary. His face and his scalp were discoloured (it was a blackish/bluish colour) and his hair had big flakes, his face was also swollen, he was looking very concerned and worried. I was also taken aback but did not want to alarm him. I just said, "don't worry in the morning when I leave work, I will make an appointment for you to see the General Practitioner (GP)." At that time there was nothing I could do as I was not expecting that to happen.

This is just another problem started, and I felt guilty going to work, but I know that in the morning, I would have to put on my thinking cap and start the process all over again. I was getting even more deflated, tired, exhausted and stress. Fortunately, those feeling and guilt only last for a short time. I am human, so I am entitled to those feelings; it's just that I do not let those feelings get to me for long. At times I would sit down and talk with my husband about Dalmar, and what more we could do to help him through the difficult time.

I also felt guilty, moaning about my weight and my waist size, when my son had the bigger problem. For me, I could go to work, go shopping and do things like that. He could not go out or do much like work or his football career. I decided to forget about my weight etc and concentrate on my son. I spoke to his dad and showed him Dalmar face and head, we tried to reassure him and let him know that it would be okay. My husband decided to take him to the Accident and Emergency department (A & E). The outcome was the same more blood test, more steroid and referral back to the General Practitioner (GP).

While driving to work that evening, I was very concerned for him, I started to cry and asked God for help, because I thought I found a cream that was helping his skin, and now another problem seemed to be arising. What should I do? I really felt sorry for him. Although I had this difficulty I still had to work. I had to try and concentrate during work because there were patients who were depending on me.

In the morning I rang the GP and booked an appointment for him. When the GP saw him, the GP was taken back and said it was an infection. The GP gave him antibiotic, steroids cream, 50/50 cream medicated shampoo. The GP also said he should try not to sweat too much or goes into the sun for long. He was also waiting for phototherapy, again.

CHAPTER TWENTY

Let me explain something, while he was waiting for his second appointment with the Dermatologist, any flare-up he had, he would have to go to the GP, and just follow the prescriptions that the Dermatologist had prescribed. The steroids cream is very strong; he would use it for two consecutive weeks and then have a break. Both the steroids cream and the 50/50 cream were making his skin worse. The 50/50 cream contains paraffin and liquid paraffin, and Dalmar asked my opinion and decided not to use it anymore.

He did not have enough skin barrier to protect him from the elements. This was 2019 and he was still had his part -time job. He was also trying to study, playing football etc. All this became too much for him and so he decided to quit his job and put his studying on hold. He said mom, "I cannot concentrate on my studies, I must allow my skin to heal first before I can move on. "

The reason he had to quit his job was because the environment was dusty and making his skin worse. Also, he had to take breaks very often, every 15 minutes, to cream his skin because it was drying out and getting itchy. This was making it very hard for him to move around and do his job properly. He was also taking sick leave from work, which he could not avoid. Both became too much as he started getting complaints, so he had to quit.

He was a good worker, even though it was a part-time job to earn his little pocket money, so he didn't have to ask his dad or me for money all the time. It was getting to him, and he did not like to go to work in that situation. He was frustrated about taking so much time off work having just started a few months. In the end he discussed it with us and came to the decision that he would have to quit.

It was a very difficult time for him, because that his little earnings, for him not to depend on us his parents, and for him to have some independence with finance.

CHAPTER TWENTY-ONE

With his head, face and hair getting infected and discoloured, he had to visit the General Practitioner again. He was given more antibiotics, steroids cream etc (different antibiotic) which work for a few days and then his skin started to break out in rashes again. With his face, hair and head getting infected it started the process again to find a cream for his face and shampoo for his hair. His scalp was very tender and felt like ulcer, it was very flaky. He kept his hair long in corn rows, but it was falling out in chunks.

It was becoming more and more difficult for me and very stressful for Dalmar. When you thought you solved one problem, another one emerged, "not good". I've brought various shampoos for eczema, but nothing worked. For his face, it was very difficult to find a face cream that was suitable. It was just more trial and error, each time I bought a cream, lotion or shampoo it might work for a while and then it was back to the drawing board. He tried different types of oil for his face, but they just did not work. His skin would start to break out again, and the rashes and oozing start all over again.

Each time he tried a cream or lotion, his skin would start to itch, get swollen, break out in rashes, and get flaky. There were not enough skin barriers to protect him, but at the end of the day he had to try the cream to see which one would work for him. Just to say, throughout the whole ordeal, I brought a tremendous amount of cream, lotions, ointments, and various products costing from hundreds to thousands of Pounds. For me the money did not matter, getting the right cream was all that mattered. I had to work all those night shifts, and when I happened to locate a cream with any potential, no matter the cost, I would buy it for him to try to see if would work.

Dalmar also tried to help by buying cream online with whatever little money he had at the time.

There were so many times when I felt like giving up, and just forgetting about his situation, but no, I just kept going and going. As mentioned earlier, I did not want him to sink into depression,
because he had just started to see improvements with some parts of his body like get his legs and back. They seemed to be getting under control with the Deprobase daily moisturising cream and then this

happened. We started to look again on the internet - Amazon, different chemist, and herbal shops etc to find some natural remedies.

I continued to spend more time at Booths Chemist again. I had to find a cream for his face, and a shampoo for his hair. This may sound easy, but no it was very difficult. Just writing about this Dark Place, is getting me upset and making me realised how stressful it was at the time for me (Just imagine my son and the things he was going through). I just continued with the process of finding different cream/ointment for his face and hair and scalp.

With his hair falling out and getting very flaky, it just added to his stress level. Therefore, I tried to be reasonable and let him know that it was not as bad as he thought, it would get better. That encouraged him to keep going. It was very bad, but I just couldn't let him know.

CHAPTER TWENTY-TWO

One day Dalmar asked me to wash his hair. Due to his hands and the tenderness of his scalp, he was having great difficult doing it. I tried to wash it, but his scalp was so flaky and tender his hair was just falling out in chunks. "How is it mom?" he asked. I just told him it was not too good.

There were bald patches all over his head and the middle was the worse, it was horrible, I just could not tell him the truth of how bad it was at the time. A year later I related to him how bad it was and told him that I could not tell him the truth at the at the time, because that would make it worse for him, as he was in a real fragile state.

I continued washing his hair, trying various kinds of shampoos. A family member told me to try the Head and shoulder shampoo, but that didn't work either. Even the eczema shampoos, of which I have brought a few different types, but they did not work. I was always back and forth to the drawing board.

At time I felt very tired, deflated, exhausted and wondering if this was going to end for him, and what else I could do. At the time of writing this book, it is over a year since this flare ups started however, it seems like a decade ago! Each time it seemed like we were getting somewhere, another flare up started, and the cycle started all over again. Writing about his problems is very difficult for me. It is a situation I would not like him to encounter again. It was really a gravely, depressive, and stressful situation.

While washing his hair, his hair was coming out in chunks, and   he has bald patches all over his head. The more I washed, the flakier it gets, it was getting to the point where it was hurting him, so I stopped and gentle use warm water.

After washing his hair, he needed an ointment for his scalp, to sooth it and to get rid of the flakes. I tried various ointments, scalp treatments; hair oils and nothing seemed to be working. He tried to take some of the antibiotic and the steroids cream, he had gotten previously from the Dermatologists, but there was no improvement, it just seemed to get worse.

One minute something worked the next it did not and then another flare up. It just continued like that.

His dad and I just try to focus on him and sometimes the other siblings got left out, but as parents we tried to let them know that for the time their brother had to be the priority because of what was happening and asked for their support.   That they had to be patient with both him and us. Sometimes when Dalmar got frustrated, he would shout at them although he did not mean to. He always apologised to us as parents or to his siblings. He once told me "Mom you don't know how bad it is for me", and I truly believe him.

Due to his hair coming out in chunks, it had to be cut to even it out. Although he is not going out, and he cover it with a Durag (a type of cloth or head cover used by youngsters). He uses it mostly at home and on rear occasions when he had to go out of the house.

The occasion when he had to go out for his appointments, his head would always be covered. He wore long trousers at home and socks to cover his feet. There were big very dark patches on his ankle and feet. He went again to the General Practitioner, who gave him a special liquid. It is mixed by adding a small drop to a litre of warm water. He used the solution to soak his feet for twenty minutes. He tried it for a few weeks/months, but it did not work. Again, it seemed like nothing was working, and each time that happened his skin got worse.

Each time I just go back to the drawing board and started all over again. At times it seems like a never-ending drama/play that just keeps going on and on. As mentioned earlier, stress and frustration continue to surface their ugly heads again.

CHAPTER TWENTY-THREE

FAMILY NIGHT

As a family, we have family game night once per week. During this time, I asked Dalmar to join in the family games night and he said "Mom, I am not up to it." During family games night we get together my husband and kids and relax at home to have real fun time. Usually, Dalmar would be in on it, we play games, we laugh, and we act silly and just have fun. I know that when he became a teenager, he was more about the phone, PlayStation and all those electronic games but we just thought he needed that bonding at that time. He would not have to focus on his condition, but just be with the family to have a laugh enjoy the togetherness.

I usually tell them how fortunate they are as when I was growing up; we did not have any electronic games or phones we had to make our own toys. However, we did not miss what we didn't have, and we enjoyed our childhood immensely. I take them on shorts journey about my childhood in my days compared to their childhood today.

As a child growing up, in the country during the summer when school was out, we had to make or find activities to do. My siblings and I as well as our cousins who lived next door and some friends, would walk for miles and spend hours picking mangoes and other fruits in the field.

We would get up early have breakfast and do our chores. We had to do our chores first, because our parents would not allow us to leave the house without doing them. One of my brothers would always sneak out without doing his chores, but when we got back my mother would be waiting for him with added chores to do.

As a child growing up, I do not recall any teenager or young person having any form of issues, or saying they were stressed or depressed and had to go to the doctor for medication, NO WAY. I am not saying kids did not have issues, but from my experience growing up in the country/rural area, I rarely ever seen or heard of kids with stress or depression. Children/young adults did not have time for those issues, they were too busy making their own entertainments.

We used to make the gig toy which my brothers, cousins and their friends would carve out of wood, it shaped like on egg. They would attach a nail at the top point, halfway in and then used a cord or a piece of string to wrap around the nail, (it would look like a yo-yo) but the gig is thrown on the ground to spin until it stopped.

I can also remember some of the bigger boys used to make their own go-cart and have their own form of racing competition. They would race from the top of the hill, and down the hill at great speed and they would race for over a mile and start again. We would watch them like it was an official mete.

My grandmother would say "those kids are going to get themselves hurt one day!". The boys would use the main road for their go-cart racing; it is the countryside therefore the amount of vehicle travelling on the road within a two-hour span was limited.

My mother and grandmother forbade us to make any go-carts or borrow from friends. My brothers however would always find a way to ride the go-cart with their friends, especially when my mother and grandmother were not around or was too busy cooking or getting other domestic chores done to notice anything, or that the boys were missing. Other times they would make up a quick excuse to go out on the road.

My mother was quick to notice that one or two kids were missing. She would question me as to their whereabouts and I would sometimes say they went to the store with our cousin because I did not want them to get in trouble. However, if they were mean to us, we would snitch and let our mother know that they went off with their friend.

There were times when we would go to get mangoes from the fields. We all have our individual baskets or bags to put our mangoes. Along with mangoes, we would pick guavas, oranges, tangerines, apples, and whatever fruits were in season. We would walk for miles breathing in the fresh air, and eating the fruits as we go along, sometimes singing songs on the way.

TWENTY-FOUR

FAMILY NIGHT- PART -TWO

We would travel through pastures, running from the cows. My brothers and cousins would climb the trees and the other cousins, and I would climb the short trees where we could reach. We had lots of laughter and fun. The fields and cow pastures are owned by family and friends, so it was okay for us children to travel from one field to another with no consequences. Also, in our group there would be a few older kids who would look after us the younger ones.

We would get home in the evenings, about5-6pm after leaving the house between 10:30-11 am. Dinner would be waiting for us. Our parents would be okay; because they knew where we were going and that there were older kids with us. We would share out the fruits with our parents and any other younger siblings who could not be on our field trip/mango walk (smile).

When it came time have our dinner, we were so filled mangoes and other fruits that we had to wait for another hour or two before we could eat. Most times my grandmother would cook red pea's soup which at the time I totally disliked. It gave us, especially me, a chance to get out of the soup dinner.

My mother caught onto us and left the soup for the next day. She would also threaten that we would not be allowed to mangoes picking again, but my grandmother would say, "Leave them alone, when they are hungry, they will have their dinner/supper. "My grandmother sometimes was easy to convince, and she would give in and sympathised with us. However, sometimes if it was extreme, like when the boys stayed out too late, then she would say, "Not this time!"

CHAPTER TWENTY-FIVE

Most times we did not have our dinner, especially when it was soup. As a child growing up I did not like soup and most of my siblings did not like it either. My grandmother was always there to the rescue of us kids when our mother got upset with us for one thing or the other.

Also, during the summer, we would go fishing catching Cray fish or shrimp. We would leave the house about 10am.Fishing was usually on a different day, we would walk for miles up the river stream, catching Cray fish under the stones. Some had very big claws and if you were not skilful, you could get bitten. I tried it once and got clawed or bitten and that was it for me. I am not skilled enough like my big brother and my cousins.

While the boys were catching the Cray fish, we girls would have a large opened-mouth bottle or tin to put their catch in. This continued for a few hours until we got home.

When we got home my brothers, cousins and their friends would go my cousin's house where they made fire outside and roast the cray fish and shrimps. They added some salt and black pepper and WALLAH!! It was delicious.

They however did the easy part of catching it, we did the hard part of carrying it all the way up and down the river. We had a wonderful time and good laughter around the fire side.

On another day, the boys would go bird hunting, and they would make their own sling shot, and they would go hunting for hours. They would come back home in the evening with their catch or sometimes none or they kept them for pets. As girls we stayed home and play shop, school and loads of different games, and made our own toys/dolls etc. During the summer we always have plenty to do.

In the country, there were limited or no electricity, especially streetlights, so when the moon was out it was one of the most beautiful sights you can imagine. At nights we would also play games, sing folk songs, and tell Anancy stories. The stories about Anancy a very cunning spider individual, who always tried to get one over on others and get them in trouble.

Anancy would always start the fire and then leave others to put it out and then he is nowhere to be found, that was how the stories of Anancy was told to us as children. (I probably told my kids a few Anancy stories but not many as they are caught up in all these electronic games etc).   Today, kids have too many activities and electronics games at their disposal and not much time to learn about cultural activities or research more into their culture.

CHAPTER TWENTY-SIX

We played games like Hopscotch, most people would know hopscotch, it is still played by youngsters today in school. There are lots more games, stories, and songs etc that we played. Some of the games we played at nights and some during the daytime.

My favourite was a game called "MOONSHINE BABY" I do not know how or where the name originated, but that was what it was called when I was growing up. This game was played during the night-time when the moon was at its fullest and very bright.

In the country area, there are practically no streetlights. There would be one at the square where everyone always gathered. A few shops around and probably one or two at various point, but where I was living there was no streetlight. The reflection of the moon on the street was wonderful, and that is when we played that game.

The game starts with someone lying at the side off-road arms open wide, feet apart looking up at the sky and then used a piece of chalk and outlined their frame, or we would put stones around the outlined frame and when we finished that person get up and you could see their shaped in the moonlight, the moonlight in the country is the most beautiful thing you could ever see or imagine, it was just bright and beautiful. We did not have any phone to take pictures, but for us it was great! We would tell stories including ghost stories and asked each other to guess riddles.

The stories would stay with me for a long time. My eldest brother was good at telling stories and most time the stories were told during the night when it was dark and scary. I remember once he told us a story about a boy called "Norman" and how he saw a ghost in the church window and heard squeaky voices, and my brother would tell the stories in a very scary voice and when he was finished, we would all run inside. After that, every time when I would attend church, I would always imagine seeing Norman through the window. It was very scary for me as a child however it was loads of fun and I enjoyed every little moment of it. That was just a little bit of my childhood memories growing up in the country during the summer.

The reason I mentioned only summer, is because school was out and growing up in the Caribbean/Jamaica is sunny all year round, and when it rains it rains a lot sometimes for a day or two.

Whenever I mentioned my childhood upbringing,

my kids would listen, fascinated, but would quickly add, "it is now the 21ˢᵗ century Mom, things changed and we have moved on", so they would literally move on (smile) and continued with their electronic devices.

That also goes for Dalmar, but I just wanted him to know that the family are with him, and we were there to support him and helped him through the terrible situation that he was going through.

I tried to explain to him that it will not last forever; there is always a light at the end of the tunnel. Saying it at the time was not easy for me but I had to be strong and reassure him constantly. For Dalmar, it was difficult because he kept having different flare upland nothing seems to be working for long. Although he was sometimes deflated, he tried to keep a level head and stayed focused.

Being a Christian family helped us overcome a lot of obstacles which this is also one of them. Even though it is focused on my son Dalmar, at the time, we all need continuous support and encouragement to deal with life's obstacles.

CHAPTER TWENTY-SEVEN

Back to Dalmar and games night, I hope you enjoy that back in time little special on summer in the country, during my childhood. As I was saying earlier, I tried to get Dalmar involved in our game's night, just to make sure he had some form of normalcy, and to focus on different things, not just in bed, or on the PlayStation or the phone. Games night we played dominoes, which I loved dearly, and I do not take any prisoners when I am playing dominoes. Dalmar loves to play dominoes, also his siblings, his dad and I taught them from they were small. He is also getting good at reading the game; his dad is very good at the game.

Domino is a very popular Caribbean game which involves four players. It can also be played as partners or "cut-throat, "as it is commonly called, which means all players for themselves. It is a very noisy and entertaining game, and when you get playing, you do not want to stop.

When I was going to school, we used to play "FRENCH DOMINOES" it also involves four players, but this time the strategy is, the more doubles you have in your hand the better the game is for you. With the normal dominoes, if you have four or more doubles in your hands then the chance of you winning is very difficult. Also, if that happen you can call for a reshuffle, which is the rule of the game.

This game I will not spend a lot of time explaining it, however, when playing in pairs or partner you want to win or dominate the game. The aim of the game is to give the other pair "Six Love" meaning they lost the game six times in a row, but when you are a skilful player, it can be very difficult to achieve.

A few years ago, I gave a friend of the family "Six Love" and he still remembers it to this day. He has been trying since to get back at me to have a replay. I am still waiting and very prepared for him (laugh).

We would also play Ludo, and different types of games, but the game I tried to get everyone involved in was the "Alphabet Games". I do not have a proper name for it, but this game Dalmar would participate in it. The reason is you sit by yourself, and he does not have to face any one like when you are playing dominoes, Ludo or any other board games. That was because he had to bandage both hands and his fingers were very sensitive and not looking their best.

Anyway, let me explain how this game is played. Because it is an alphabetical game, we start from the beginning by saying the letter of the alphabet. Each player would have a piece of paper with the headings - BOY, GIRL, PLACE, ANIMAL, FOOD, THING, and the end column TOTAL. Each column scored out of ten and at the end of game the total should be sixty. If two or more of the players get the same answer, they would split the points and they would get five points each. If they cannot find an answer for any of the column, then it would be zero.

If five of us playing the game it can started from left or right, but in this instance, I am going to start from the right, I will be in charge of this round from my right, I would ask the person to start to say the alphabet from the beginning but not say it out loud, and then I would instruct him or her either go fast, slow, or medium because I am in control of the game. I would say to the person to start saying the alphabet medium, I will tell that person when to stop, and asked what letter they stopped at.   For example, if the person stopped
on the letter "D" all players would start including the person who just said the alphabet. A boy name beginning with "D" example Derrick, girl = Daisy, Place=Denmark,   animal=Dog,   food=donut   and thing=desk, the total=sixty points.

However, at this point, this is where the game gets better, because I oversee this first round, therefore I am in control of the game, so when I finish all my six columns, the other players would have thirty to sixty seconds to complete their column, after sixty seconds all pens down, even if they have not completed their column.

The rules are set at the beginning of the game, so it can be thirty seconds or sixty seconds, to make it more competitive and more fun with thinking. I would ask the other players to tell what they have for boy, girl etc. If two or more players have the same for any of the column, then it would be five points each. It sounds easy, but when you are on a fast tract the first name that comes to mind you just write it down, therefore most players would end up with the same names for boy, girl, and so forth.

Each player gets their turn to oversee the game and so it continues. Some players will write down unusual names especially for animal and thing, but a dictionary is present or Google, and if the name is not in the dictionary or on Google it is a zero. Sometimes my younger son and my daughter used name from the Annamae character and Naruto which sometimes can be acceptable, if all agreed on it.

If ten games are played at the end of the game, the player that adds up the most point wins and go down the line, some players might end up with a tie. That in a nutshell is the alphabet game. I liked to play with the family, and we always have a barrel of laughter and fun. As stated earlier it is a fun game to get all the family involved and to have a good laugh.

During the COVID-19 Pandemic and lockdown, my family from America used to have zoom time every week and this is one of the games we would play along with others. We would all have a good laugh. It also brought the family together.

CHAPTER TWENTY-EIGHT

Just a little back-track about games night with the family, this is just to let you know that I tried to have my son keep up family activities and be involved with his siblings. Having those games nights, I knew would keep his mind off his situation and not get too depressed. It would also cause him not to cut himself off totally from the family. He also had a few friends that he talked to over the phone, but I do not think he told them how bad his situation was at the time.

Although having games night helped him to have some form of normalcy, and interaction with the family, we were still back to the situation of finding him a cream/shampoo for his head, face, and the rest of his body. I found a cream that was helping him with his feet, trunks, thighs and back but his face, head and hair needed a different cream, ointment, and shampoo.

This situation sometimes seemed like a never-ending problem, I brought creams, lotions, ointments, shampoos, and oils of different brands. Some were from natural remedies, some I brought on-line mostly on Amazon, others I brought from different pharmacies/drug stores and the list goes on.

I remember one time I brought this special ointment in a small tube which cost £25.00. I am thinking this must be good for the price and the size of the cream/ointment.

However, this was not the case, because a few hours after using the ointment, Dalmar's skin started to break out again in spots and became itchy. He had to stop applying the ointment to his skin and this was getting very frustrating for him. Every time I brought a new product/cream which I thought could help him, it just made his skin worse.

During those little moments that is when I felt like I could go any further and just felt like giving up, but there was always that tiny little fighting spirit left and that little voice that says do not give up yet, just keep trying. If I gave up on him, who would be there to help him, and if he thought his mother could not cope with his problems anymore that might just cause him to sink deep into depression.

Having setbacks like those can be very devasting at times, as it felt like nothing was going to help him. The prospect seemed dark and dull. It happened a lot where we brought a cream/ointment or lotion and thought it would work, but nothing happened, and that was how it had been going for the duration of his problems. During those times I would bring a product home, just to find something that work no matter the cost. It was always going to be trial and error and not the cost.

The cost for me was not relevant, it was getting him better and no matter how expensive the cream/lotion cost if it would help him then I would buy it. I remember buying a cream and when he read the ingredients he stated, "I don't want that one." I could not bring it back to the chemist, because that chemist did not take back certain product, when it left the shop, especially in the time of COVID-19 Pandemic.

Dalmar has been on this road to recovery, with tremendous help from his dad and me. We have been with him every step of the way. With all this trial on error, and after trying a tremendous number of products, I finally found a cream for his skin, and the shampoo which is the "ginger shampoo." I brought it from the Body Shop, and he is still using that shampoo today.

With his face however, it was difficult. His eyebrow faded out; it had no hair due to the bad flare-ups. If he started to sweat, his forehead would itch and burning, so that was another problem/situation we were faced with. I was told about the Manuka honey and search internet about the benefits. I went out and brought it from Holland and Barrett shop.

He had to spread it over his face and leave it on for twenty minutes then wash it off. He was doing it for a few weeks, until eventually his face started to get back its colour and the itchiness started to gradually fade. He is slowly on the road to recovery.

EPILOGUE/CONCLUSION

PART ONE

Its March 2022, Dalmar had been in that "**DARK PLACE**" for over two and a half years. He has been gradually coming out of that place with lots of help and support from his dad, his siblings and myself. Even though it is a medical situation, I would not want it to happen to him again. Without our help, it could have been very devastating. I am happy that his dad and I were there for him every step of the way, to support, guide and encourage him.

During those times, I tried to help him as much as I could, I made sure he was mentally, physically, emotionally, and spiritually stable, talking to him listening to him. There were times his dad and I would sit for hours talking to him and more than anything listening to him. It helped him because he knew we were there for him. Dalmar also started to visit the park daily, to do his training and exercise, due to the fact we were still in lock down.

The impact and strain it had on the family especially me, was very hard. Going to work and working various nights' shifts were having an impact on my health, physically and emotionally which left me at times mentally drained. Sometimes I also felt as if I was neglecting the rest of the family to focus on him.

The reason I was so laser focused on him is because I wanted to make sure it did not affect him mentally or have him sink into deep depression. He was already stressed and depressed, and that was a very difficult time for him. In the future, he will be able to look back and really talk about this **"DARK PLACE** "with others who might be experiencing similar situation. He will be able to give mental and emotional support because he overcomes the worse which made him stronger.

Talking and listening to him continuously served to remind him that we were there for him, and it helped him to stay focus. Both his dad and I continue to guide him and remind him that we would always be there.

He is now out of that dark place never to return, which will make him stronger. His dad and I along with his siblings are still focus on Christ, who has been our Rock throughout this ordeal. After being in that **"DARK PLACE"** for over two and a half years, his total being is now well tuned, he can now focus on the things he wanted to do all along like his football and his studies. All those things that were put aside during his time in that dark place.

I told Dalmar he should ensure that he attends church as often as possible. I always remind myself that God is the centre of my universe and with God, I can overcome all obstacles.

I tried to impart that to my kids so that their foundation in Christ will always be strong. They were taught to be respectful to others and all those values that make them valuable contributors to society.

With this experience, he has a lot to impart. I would always listen to his suggestion and even try some of them to see if they worked or not, and that is getting him involved with his treatment.

After various trials of different creams, ointments etc, the cream we finally found that helped his skin was the **Diprobase Daily Moisturising Cream**. This cream is very compatible with his skin, and he does not have any negative reactions to it. He is still using the cream today.

For his hair, he continues using the Ginger shampoo brought from the body shop and the conditioner, and he also continues using the castor oil to moisturise his scalp. He has done a patch test after the second ease out of lock down and was able to get the appointment to do the patch testing. (This is to test over fifty products on his skin (50) to ascertain if he is allergic to any of the products.) At the time of his appointment, his skin was clearing up and in good condition for the testing.

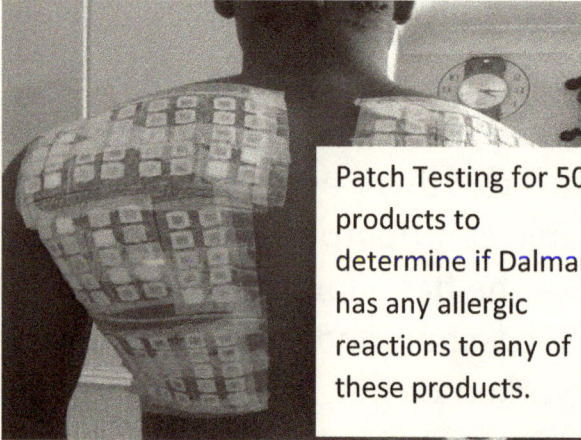

Patch Testing for 50 products to determine if Dalmar has any allergic reactions to any of these products.

He had to keep the patches on his skin for over two days before going back to do another set of testing for the same time. They all came back negative. Interestingly, during the testing the consultant and the other doctors were appalled as to why he needed testing, but when I showed them a few pictures of his skin in the early days, they just could not believe it. I am very happy with the results and Dalmar is beaming with happiness, that the flare up of his eczema had nothing to do with allergies. It all happened due to stress. Stress can be fatal and destructive if not handled early with the proper help and support.

Stress also comes in different forms, and for him it was due to his football training, games peer pressure and what he thought was the overall expectations of him. He normally pushes himself to the limited. Failure for him is just a setback; he always strives for goal believing that one should not give up. Doing his studies and football, he tries to do his best.

Although he would not consider himself a perfectionist, he is always aiming towards perfection. Most kids want their parents to be proud of them. We always tell him, "Dalmar, we only want your best and that is good enough."

I told him his dad and I are proud of him, and we are there to helped and support him. Trying to push himself very hard and trying to prove himself to me and his dad, we told him to do his best because that is all we can asked for as parents. We will always continue to give him guidance and

support whenever he asks for it, or we see that he needs it.

EPILOGUE/CONCLUSION

PART -TWO

As parents his dad and I always told him "We are here to support you in whatever field of study or training you are doing. You should not feel pressured by anything or anyone", sometimes as young teenagers/young adult, peer pressure can play a vital part in stress.

I hope you enjoyed reading "Coming out of a Dark Place." Dalmar has finally completed most of his study and got his certificates. He also continues doing other studies in the field of health and fitness.

Dalmar is now a semi-pro footballer. He suffered a major injury to his right knee during a football match, in February 2022 when he collided with his goalkeeper. He sustained fracture to his Medial Collateral Ligament (MCL), ruptured his Anterior Cruciate Ligament (ACL), two Meniscus
Tears and Bone Bruising, but that's how the game of football works. That is a very big setback for Dalmar again, just imagined just getting over a medical

problem which lasted for over two and a half years and then just as he started to get back on his feet and into his career this injury happened. It is now June 2022, and he is still recovering.

The injuries he suffered is bad, he was on crutches for a few weeks. Coming out of that dark place, has helped him to grow in strength mentally, emotionally, and spiritually. It is helping him to cope with his injuries.

Being at home for over four months with crutches is not easy for him, especially after what he went through just over two and a half years ago.

As mother I was very concerned for him, as I knew it can be stressful, especially he just reached that level of football. He just started a full-time job in a sporting and health environment in West Bromwich and then here comes another setback. I did not want him to get stressed about it. However, he is very much focused this time, and as usual his dad and I talked to him and are there to support him.

Now he can drive, go to the gym but he still must take it one day at a time. He is socializing with families and friends and focusing on getting better. He did an MRI scan, and his recovery process is going great, he will have to do surgery to get back to the level of football he used to play.

He is going back to the gym and has consultation and physiotherapy twice weekly. His skin is back to normal, and he continues to use the products. He can also wear all different types of clothing, including spandex material. Although he still focuses on mostly cotton material for certain clothing, especially bedding. He still avoids dusty environment or dusty places.

He can go swimming and he started to played football to strengthen his knee while he awaits surgery. His full-time job also associated with football and Health Environment is also trying to strengthen his knee by involving in football practice and gym. However, nothing heavy, he still must wait for his surgery dates. His studying is going great which is still online however, he must do face to face for any practical sessions, which he has done a few.

Dalmar finally had his surgery done in September 2022, and the surgery went well, he is having weekly physiotherapy sessions. The healing process will be long, but it will get him back to the level of his football career.

At the time of completing this book, the world has just been jolted with the passing of Her Majesty Queen

Elizabeth 11. She passed away at 96 years of age. I can remember shopping in Curry's store at about1 9:10, my husband and myself, were in the TV isle and I remember hearing Her Majesty name mentioned in the past tense. I stood still not sure what to make of it, as I was looking at the television screen.

I beckoned to my husband to come closer, and then it was announced again. It was such a shock, totally unexpected. The impact that she has had on the commonwealth and the world at large over her seventy plus year reign, was made even more stark as country after country paid tribute to her and her work.

She started public life at the young age of 21 and has been faithful to her duties to the very end. Most notably, she installed the newly elected Prime Minister of England, two days before she passed. The Queen left a legacy that will be entrenched in the lives of both the Royal family as well as the millions of lives she touched through her unflinching and unwavering commitment to the monarchy.

Her son King Charles 111 will ascend the throne in short order while the world waits in anticipation of what the future holds. May her soul rest in peace and light perpetual shine upon her. Long live the King. It's now October 2022, and my son is doing great, the healing process is fantastic, he is all smiles, and that is wonderful. He will be back to his level of football by next season; he continues his studies towards his career goal.

My weight and health issues are now back on track, after a long process, and it is a continuing phase, I have a YouTube channel, (my weight loss journey during lockdown 2020) along with my first book published. I've also done a few healthy videos and I'm continuing my weight loss journey and maintaining my weight.

It's now the end of October 2022 and Dalmar is finally getting towards his career goal, I hope he will continue to achieve his goal, although life is not a bed of roses and anything can happen, he is just taking things one day at a time.

STRESS

WHAT IS STRESS? According to the Collins English Dictionary, it is tension or strain, **stressed-out suffering from tension. OXFORD DICTIONARY STATES STRESS**, as a state of mental or emotional strain or tension resulting from adverse or demanding circumstances. "He obviously under a lot of stress".

Stress comes in different form, and if overwhelmed by it can caused mental issued, some people seek help early others try to hide it or think it's nothing until it manifests upon them, and sometimes it's too late to help that individual, and sometimes they refuse help, stating that they are okay, and it's nothing to worry about. If society can be more vigilant, and try to be there for our families, friends, neighbours, and colleagues, see signs of mental issues/stress and depression, they can be guided to visit their Doctor/GP or therapy, before it's too late.

Be cognizant and try to help more people out there, before they sink into deep depression, which sometime can lead to suicide or suicidal tendency. Some people must be on long-term medications because it affects them mentally, physically, and emotionally. The medications help them to continue to live and perform life as much as they can, being a part of society, and to have some form of normalcy.

This book is not just about my son illness and his time in that dark place, but for me, I just want to share with people out there in our society today, that no matter what you are going through, there's always light at the end of the tunnel. At times, some people just want to be left alone or just be by themselves, but that is not good, try and find at least one person to communicate with and share your feelings; try not to think what people are going to say, or criticise your illness. Try not to think that you will be judged by your situation/illness. Be honest and practical, and if people are willing to help let them help.

One of the things that makes life in general so interesting is the turns it can take and how it can prove to be both surprising and interesting at the same time. This journey took Dalmar in and out of "THE DITCH" and despite the fact that he did not achieve his dream of being a professional football player, he still did not give up. Life took him in a slightly different direction. He began playing again at a semi-pro level, and has recently launched is own business as a Fitness Training

Instructor with tremendous support from his family and friends, and with God's help.

Dalmar showed that you can get knock down a few times, but if you exhibit the will and fortitude that is within you, you can get back up again. Life is both about challenges and rewards and if we have the right approach, attitude, and mindset, it can be a rewarding journey.

Today, Dalmar is very vibrant, happy, young adult, and enjoying life, he continues his studying, working, training very hard and going to the gym. Being with his family and friends makes him happy. Please check him out@dynamicstrength/www.instagram.com/dynamics trength.

Thank you for reading my book and please share with your friends and family.

www.ingramcontent.com/pod-product-compliance
Lightning Source LLC
LaVergne TN
LVHW011400080426
835511LV00005B/369